Bollywood

Iris Howden

Consultant: Barbara Singh

Published in association with The Basic Skills Agency

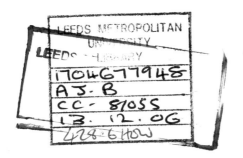
The Publishers would like to thank the following for permission to reproduce copyright material:

Photo credits
pp.iv, 10, 16, 20 © British Film Institute; p.8 © RK Films/The Kobal Collection; p.23 © Sippy Films/The Kobal Collection; p.26 © Dave Benett Getty Images.

Orders: please contact Bookpoint Ltd, 130 Milton Park, Abingdon, Oxon OX14 4SB. Telephone: (44) 01235 827720. Fax: (44) 01235 400454. Lines are open from 9.00–6.00, Monday to Saturday, with a 24-hour message answering service. Visit our website at www.hoddereducation.co.uk.

© Iris Howden 2005
First published in 2005 by
Hodder Murray, a member of the Hodder Headline Group
338 Euston Road
London NW1 3BH

Impression number   10 9 8 7 6 5 4 3 2 1
Year   2010 2009 2008 2007 2006 2005

Cover photo © Nils Jorgensen/Rex Features. *Bombay Dreams* at the Apollo Victoria Theatre, London, 2002.
Typeset in 14pt Palatino by SX Composing DTP, Rayleigh, Essex.
Printed in Great Britain by CPI Bath.

A catalogue record for this title is available from the British Library

ISBN-10 0 340 90053 9
ISBN-13 978 0 340 90053 6

Contents

Poster for the film, *Mother India*.

1 What is Bollywood?

In India, people love going to the cinema.
Every village, town and city has one.
Most people go to see a film every week.
Some go more often.
Millions of people all over the country
want to see the latest films.
If they like a film they will see it twice
or even three times.

Indian audiences don't just watch the films.
They show their feelings as they watch.
They stamp and shout.
They cheer the hero and boo the villain.
They whistle when a sexy dance is shown.
Sometimes they throw coins at the screen
to show how much they like the film.

The films they flock to see are the ones
we in the West call 'Bollywood' films.
More serious films are made in India
but Bollywood films are fun.
They appeal to the whole family.

They are a mixture of romance, action,
comedy, song and dance.
This is known as 'masala' which means
a mixture of spices in cooking.

Bollywood is a name made up in the 1980s.
It is like Hollywood in India.
Other big cities have film studios.
The most famous film studios are in Mumbai.
The old name for Mumbai is Bombay.

About 800 full-length films are made
in India every year.
In that country there are people
of many different religions,
such as Hindus, Muslims, Buddhists and Sikhs.
They speak 15 different languages.
So the films have to appeal to everyone.

Bollywood is the centre of Hindi film-making.
It doesn't matter if the audience does not
speak Hindi.
Bollywood films are always easy to follow.
The plots are stories about good and evil.
The action is fast-moving with plenty of fights.
There is also lots of singing and dancing.
These films are made not only for the people
who live in India but for everyone.

Millions of Indian people who live in Britain
and other countries enjoy Bollywood films.
For many it is a way of keeping in touch
with their roots.
It's a link with India and the Indian way of life.

Now these films have been shown on TV.
Non-Asian people enjoy them too.

Bollywood films make people feel good.

2 Films Through the Ages

In many ways Bollywood has copied Hollywood.
In the 1920s, a man called D.G. Phalke
set up the first film company in India.
He made silent films, full of action.
They had lots of special effects.
The plots were based on old stories
about Indian gods, kings and queens.
Everyone knew them so they were easy
to follow.

At that time, few Indian women went into acting.
It was not thought to be a job for a decent girl.
Phalke had to cast a young male actor
as the queen.
Nowadays, male actors still dress up as women
but only in the comic parts of a film.

In early films, music was played on a piano
as the film was shown.
Later, people wanted to hear the actors speak.
The Jazz Singer was the first US 'talkie'.
It was made in 1927.
The first Indian film with sound came out
four years later.
It was called *Alam Ara*. It caused a riot.
People fought to get tickets.

With sound, music could be added.
Singing and dancing became an important
part of the film.

In the 1930s, films were more about real life.
Some of the same story lines are used today.
One favourite is the love triangle with
two men in love with the same girl.
This was the theme of *Devdas* made in 1935.
It became a classic and has been re-made twice.

By now, women were acting in films.
The way their lives were changing was shown.
Some films had the heroine refusing to marry
her parents' choice of husband.

In the 1930s, there were many studios.
Each had its own stars.
After the war some of the top actors,
such as Raj Kapoor, set up their own companies.

Many think that film-making
reached its peak in the 1950s.
Some people call it the Golden Age.
In 1952, India held its first Film Festival.
People from the West began to take notice.
Films were dubbed into other languages
and sold abroad.

Films of that time record the changes
coming about in India.
People moved to live in the big cities.
They found it hard to cope.
The poor people left in the villages
also had a difficult time.
Mother India was made in 1957.
It was about one woman's struggle to survive.
It was very moving and became a major hit.

The set for the film, *Awaara*, in 1951.

The 1960s brought a lighter touch.
Rock and roll came to India.
Films were in colour with up-beat songs.
Costumes and settings were lavish so
the cost of making a film became very high.

Soon there was a split between directors.
Some, like Satyajit Ray, wanted to make
more serious films,
the kind we call 'Art' films.
They branched out to form
what was known as 'New Cinema'.
Others went for box office success.

In the 1970s, films became more violent.
Story lines were often about gangsters
and crime in the big cities.
Horror films were made in the 1980s.
These put off the family audience.
So directors went back to making love stories
with happy endings,
the kind of film we know as 'Bollywood'.

Hrithik Roshan in *Kabhi Khushi Kabhie Gham*.

3 Heroes and Villains

The hero is at the centre of every Bollywood movie.
He has to be tall, dark and handsome
– an action man who can use his fists,
ride and shoot.
He also has to be a really nice guy,
the kind of young man any mother would like
her daughter to marry.

The actor who can fill this role
can earn very high fees.
Often a film won't go ahead until the director
can sign up a top male star.
Indian actors tend to become type-cast.
Some actors always play the hero.
Others are always cast as the villain.

Raj Kapoor, Dilip Kumar and Dev Anand (Kumar)
were three actors with sex appeal.
From the 1950s on, they starred in many hit films.
The 1960s' craze for rock and roll
made a star of Raj's brother, Shammi.
He was young and modern.
He could dance really well.

In the 1970s, Rajesh Khanna had many offers
of marriage from female fans.
Today, there is even more fan worship.
TV programmes and fan magazines
give all the latest gossip about the stars.

Fans copy their clothes and their hair styles.
They are mobbed when they appear in public.
In modern times, Salman Khan, Aamir Khan,
(who are not related), Amitab Bachan
and Shah Rukh Khan have become superstars.
Hrithik Roshan is the next up-and-coming star.

The hero has to have a good speaking voice.
In the early days sound was recorded on set.
Nowadays, it is added later, so the actor
can put more feeling into his lines.

If he can't sing, a good singer's voice is used.
The actor will mime to the songs on screen.
The artists who record the songs are called
'play back' singers.

Sound effects are an important part of the film.
The audience expects the hero to win
but he has to put up a good fight.
Fights last for a long time in Bollywood movies.
The loud sound effects add to the excitement.

Older, less good-looking actors play the villains.
The ideal villain has a deep voice.
He can chill people with a word
or fix them with an evil stare.

Quite often the villain is rich.
He can offer the girl more money.
In early films he might have been
a landlord or a mill owner.
Sometimes he was a member of the family,
an evil cousin or a heavy-handed father.
He did wicked things and tried to stop
the hero and heroine from getting together.

Villains have been updated over the years.
In the 1970s, they were often gangsters
or criminals.
By the 1980s, they could be serial killers.
Nowadays, the fight between good and evil
is not so clear cut.

Amjad Khan in *Sholay*.

Values have changed in real life
so films have become more complex.

Quite often, the villain is the person
the audience remembers best.
Amjad Khan, the villain in *Sholay*
made in 1975, was one of these.
Actors like him worked hard at being
really creepy 'baddies'.

In some cases there was a price to pay.
It spilled over into their private lives.
Some actors who played the villain
were shouted at in the street.
They were even pelted with stones.
In the 1950s, people stopped calling
their baby boys Pran.
This was because an actor of that name
was so nasty on screen.

Stars are not made for life by one success.
Two bad films in a row often means the end
of their career.
They try to pick a winner when choosing a part.

4 Good Girls and Bad Ones

The heroine has to be young and pretty.
Apart from falling in love with the hero,
she does not have to do a great deal.
She often has a lot to put up with
so she must be able to express
pain and suffering.
Meena Kumari was an actress who could do this.
She played many tragic roles.
She was often seen as the ideal Indian woman,
the sort who upheld family values.

Actresses were often paired up
with the same actors in their films.
As couples, they were a box office draw.
Quite often an actress was known
only by her first name or by a nickname
such as 'Baby' Rani.

Older actresses go on to play the mother.
This is an important role as the hero
is always shown as being close to his mother.

The heroine does not appear in bedroom scenes.

Most actresses refuse to kiss on screen.
Sexy movements in the dancing
give spice to the film.
The heroine can get her sari wet
to show off her figure,
but she is very much a good girl –
the kind her family would be proud of.

Aishwarya Rai in *Devdas*.

In the past, many actresses were trained dancers.
If they can't sing, a 'play back'
singer's voice is used.
The most famous of these is called Lata.
She has recorded thousands of songs for films.

Nowadays, looks are more important.
Actresses have often been models or beauty queens
before becoming film stars.
Aishwarya Rai and Shushmita Sen
are two who made this move.
Today, soaps on Indian TV set the fashions.
Scenes which are meant to be dreams are popular.
In these the heroine wears stylish clothes.
Her hair and make-up are perfect.

Actresses who play the bad girl can drink,
smoke and wear skimpy clothes.
The mothers and grandmas in the audience
enjoy shaking their heads at such goings on.
In early films, these girls were dancing girls.
Later, they became city types or gangsters' molls.
Nowadays, they are often spoiled rich girls.

The bad girl gets to sing good songs.
She may be 'the other woman'
or just a good friend to the hero.

Often she has to die before the movie ends.
One actress, famous for playing this kind of part,
was called Helen.
She was a very good Hindi dancer
and had a lot of male fans.
They used to call her 'H Bomb'.

Sometimes the bad female is a wicked
mother-in-law or step-mother.
Older actresses often really enjoy playing these parts.
They can go over the top with their acting.

H Bomb in *Sholay*.

5 East Meets West

Cable TV in India has not meant the end
of Hindi films.
If anything, it has made them more popular.
TV and films feed off each other.
Programmes such as quiz shows
and talent contests
are spin-offs from the films.
Others give fashion news and gossip
about the stars.
These are also popular.

Music is very important in Hindi films.
DJs in clubs and on the radio plug
the latest songs from the films.
If the songs catch on, the film will be a hit.
Here in Britain, the radio station Club Asia
brings new sounds to Asian and non-Asian youth.

In 2004, Channel 4 ran a competition.
The prize was to act as an extra
in a Bollywood film.
Over 1,000 young people applied.
Six of them reached the finals
and made the trip to Mumbai.
They acted before a live Indian audience.
The winner was Rupak Mann.
She won a small part in a movie.

Bombay Dreams, a Bollywood musical co-written by Meera Syal.

Channel 4 has also shown a series
of Indian films.
Audiences enjoyed the drama of Hindi films.
They loved the dance routines.
In these, groups of up to 100 dancers
perform with many changes of costume.
The BBC has also used a Hindi group of dancers
as a link between programmes.

British-born stars Meera Syal and
Sanjeev Bhaskar are well known on TV.
Their comedy shows 'Goodness Gracious Me'
and 'At Home With the Kumars' are a big success.
Now a new wave of talent is coming in.

Gurinder Chadha, the female director,
had a hit with *Bend It Like Beckham*.

Her new movie is a Bollywood type of film.
The plot is based on Jane Austen's novel
Pride and Prejudice.
It is about an Indian family trying
to marry off their daughters,
and it is called *Bride and Prejudice*.
The female lead is Aishwarya Rai,
a top star in India.
This may be her chance to become
as well known in the West as in the East,
and to make the move from Bollywood
to Hollywood.